YOUR FINANCIAL CHECKUP

THE PRESCRIPTIONS TO MAILBOX MONEY

BY DR. KING MCCRAY, PH.D.

For William & Rondalin:

Thank you for allowing me to fail, learn from my mistakes, and create a path to success. There is no me without you and I am always appreciative of that.

Table of Contents

Introduction

M ost will take the "normal" approach in life. They'll finish high school, go to college, get a good 9-5 job, retire with some ease and comfort, and call it a day. Then there are the outliers. The "different ones". The individuals who simply want more out of life and more out of their experience. They seek just a little more risk, a little more reward, and have their eyes set on a higher peak that they know can be obtained.

That's who *you* are!

That's why you decided to read this book because you know there's more to your money and what you want. This is your second look at what you're doing and how you can take it to the next level. There is a peace of mind when knowing money is readily available when needed. If you're reading this, you are either a business owner, serial entrepreneur, an overworked employee looking for change, or simply an individual who would like to add another stream of income to their success. If you've been looking for ways to generate passive income, this is a financial check-up you'll want to be on time for. This guide will provide you with many different options, some of which will require start-up capital while other options will only require your time and effort (which is worth more than you know), but all will lead you to the end result: Mailbox Money!

Whether you want to be able to free yourself from the daily grind and still generate a full-time income, spend more time with family and friends while traveling the world, or becoming one of the illustrious "debt free" — passive income is *THE* key!

Passive income is any income that requires *little* or no ongoing work to maintain. Ideally, you want your passive income business(es) to require very little work to maintain, but occasionally you may want to increase your money by expanding on your passive income opportunities, or by combining more than one.

You can always outsource these tasks by leveraging the proper relationships and eliminate them from your own schedule as well. One of the biggest things I learned from a mentor is the power of *leverage*. Leverage relationships. Leverage connections. Leverage social media. Leverage employees. Leverage whatever is going to have you meet that final comfort you seek financially.

During this check-up, we'll discuss the top tips and strategies the wealthy are using for creating streams of passive income, while also growing your knowledge of opportunities that you may not have thought of, so you can enjoy a true Financial Prescription for Confidence. Wealth isn't always about money, but it feels damn good to know that you have it coming in *consistently*.

What is Mailbox Money?
Passive income, duh!

Passive income, often known as "side hustles" or, mailbox money, are simply one of those ways to quickly add to your income so that you can pay off credit card debt, save for a large purchase, increase your retirement funds, or even reduce your personal financial stress. The most popular type of side hustle is the passive income *streams* where you have many sources of income that make up your side hustle. With this way of living, you create your mailbox money (or many) additional revenue streams by taking on low-effort and low-investment projects that end up making loads of profits. No, it isn't too good to be true, but are you willing to do the work? There are plenty of people who *want* to be wealthy, but they don't *want* to do the work to get there!

Passive income isn't a magic button. It takes time and effort. It involves putting in some proper work and building a real business that will create long-term income. If you're willing to put in your time and your money to the prescriptions outlined below, you can be making an income quickly for years to come, without ever touching your savings account. For example, most real estate investments make up a form of passive income! That's literally waking up to money every single day.

However, real estate and rental properties are just two of the most common passive investments. Another great way to earn passive income is through stock investments, but there truly are endless kinds of passive income streams– from laundromats and vending machines to Amazon Kindle Publishing and online courses!

Passive income refers to any income earned in an area that doesn't require too much work. For instance, there are many passive income generating activities that involve a fair amount of effort, but in the long run, they still make money even if the original owner isn't around – yes, that's you. The passive income streams that can be most profitable and easiest to create are those that involve selling products online usually because the investment needed is lower as there are few overhead costs.

The truth is that it doesn't take much at all to start an income earning stream if you are ready to spend some time learning the different ways to harness it– and considering that your hands have landed on this book, you clearly are! Time is a true invaluable possession and it's one we cannot get back. Passive income is usually (not always) earned without much or no effort at all. But you still have to harness your own time and effort to build something that becomes self-regulating.

"If you are not willing to learn, no one can help you. If you are determined to learn, no one can stop you."

-Zig Ziglar

"Why should I care about mailbox money?"
Wait....what?!

The benefits of passive income are plentiful. First, this type of income allows you to set your own schedule. Flexibility and work-life balance should be a huge factor for anyone thinking about getting away from where they are. Enjoying your family while you earn money is a no-brainer! Secondly, it allows for control in your working life because you get to choose which projects and streams you are most interested in, and therefore what you want to focus on. Third, it allows you to be your own boss! This equates to the ability to better manage your time while at the same time earning money and not being stuck with a company that you don't feel is paying you what you're *worth!* Financial net worth is important and something everyone should know. If you don't know *what* your net worth is then you absolutely need to continue to read and find that answer. Finally, it gives you an opportunity to offset tax liability and gives you freedom to invest freely with "F-U Money!" That hit the spot, huh?

A few key benefits of a passive income stream are the potential to increase your standard of living, obtain financial confidence that you may not have had before, and prepare you for your future. The main reason why people struggle to generate passive income is because they fail to identify the best opportunities, or because they want to jump to the end result without putting the work in. As I tell my clients in our Discovery Calls, *"We're at Point A, you already see Point Z, but in order to get there we have to go through the rest of the process."* Some of what you read are things you have already heard before, but why haven't you acted on it? No direction? No accountability? There will be things you learn here that will allow you to leverage and create all those.

Other benefits of passive income include the fact that you have the opportunity to work in a variety of fields. This means that you can diversify your skills and interests. For example, one of the benefits of investing in online courses is that you can earn a living by getting paid to teach others things you are completely passionate about. You have the potential to make a bigger income with a greater number of projects as well, and unlike many think, this doesn't mean that it requires a lot more time from you! Instead, it means that you get to set up all kinds of projects and can simultaneously enjoy the benefits (a.k.a. the money) all while working very little.

When thinking of passive income in the form of earning, it is important to remember that you will not always get rich right away. If you do not follow the prescriptions laid out and the guidance closely enough or if you do not maximize the opportunities, you may not make much money at all– that's especially true if you give up too quickly. With the right moves, however, you may find yourself in a better situation financially, and you may just have the opportunity to be a part of the 1% of the population that owns 44% of the wealth in the world!

Prescription: Monetize Your Possessions
You have what they need

How much are you worth? That's what I ask a lot of my clients on our first call. Seriously, how much are you worth? No lie, 9 times out of 10, I hear *"I'm priceless."* And then I have to go and correct them by saying, *"If that were true, your job wouldn't put a value on you."* You can literally hear a pin drop, but it's the truth. Your job wouldn't put a value on you if you were truly priceless. You wouldn't pay car insurance, life insurance, dental insurance, home owners insurance, etc., if you were priceless. The bank would not ask you what you own or look at your debt to see if something is within your financial reach if it were so. This is how I want you look at yourself from now on: To *someone* you are worth *something* and you have what they *need*.

What do you *have* that is of value? Realizing that your possessions, whether internally or externally, is of value and can be monetized will help you on your journey to mailbox money. Worldly possessions are one of the main sources to success in the world of passive income. Whether it's tangible or not, there is value in what you possess and what you own So, look in the mirror or look around, because what you have is worth plenty.

Real Estate — Active

"*Owning property is beneficial for any individual who wants to create an additional stream of income.*" Yup, you heard it here first people! Now, notice I didn't say owning a *home*, but I used the word property. Property can be defined as many different things, but the root is that it's an asset. One of the main assets that most of the wealthy own is tangible property (i.e. homes, land, etc.) Not everyone isn't meant to be a homeowner and not all people can properly own homes — read that again. When we start to think about ownership, and our possessions, one of the main things we can equate that to is owning some type of property. Owning a property in real estate has two sides to it: Active & Passive. Both play a pivotal role in what you're trying to accomplish, but each have their own time commitment and resources used. Rental properties are a proven method for generating passive income, but it comes with some definitive risks. As a fiduciary, I recommend that you determine three things before getting started:

- How much return do you want from your investment?
- What total costs and expenses will you incur from this investment?
- What financial risks are you running with this investment?

In addition, this is one of the passive income streams that does require periodic injections of cash for upkeep of the property. You need to be realistic with your expected returns as well. In other words, this isn't something you can completely outsource, though, there are opportunities to hand over a majority of the duties. As a landlord, or property owner, there are certain things you can indeed outsource. For example, you can outsource maintenance tasks to a third party company so as to limit the amount of time and effort you need to spend on something. You could also outsource the entire investment to a property management company, but this could potentially eat into your profit. It is more about what you want to make and how you want to obtain that amount. This is exactly why you need to know what you are passionate about. If what you like to do is to spend time in an active role and mostly focusing on the money-making aspect of things, make sure to outsource the steps that you really don't like, such as the painting of your real estate or keeping-up with the grass. But don't be fooled– you cannot just outsource all tasks without keeping track of the quality and the costs. Always remember, it's quality over quantity. Don't end up investing just to be stuck with problems and bills on your hands.

Similarly, you can't reasonably expect to charge thousands of dollars in monthly rent in a less-desirable neighborhood. Be reasonable, be aware, and do your research before you invest in real estate.

If you want to start investing in rental properties, I recommend networking with individuals through *Bigger Pockets* (a Real Estate investing community), doing a lot of research online using software like *PropStream*, and checking out the properties yourself to be sure you're getting exactly what you're paying for. Make sure to know what you are investing in before– hire the right profess   ionals to do an evaluation of the property before you sign anything. Sometimes, the electrical wires may be faulty, or you may end up investing in something that is more trouble than something you can benefit from. The key is to *earn* a return on your investment (ROI).

Diversification is an important part of any investment portfolio.

This simply means that it is better to invest in real estate with a wide variety. By doing this, you can spread your risk and reduce the possibility that any of your investments will lose value. Diversification is the best way of ensuring that you do not lose all of your money when the market takes a bad turn. One of the best ways to diversify in real estate is through rental properties, including commercial units, an apartment complex, condos, or a duplex, strip malls, RV units, and more. Since rental properties generally go up and down in value this provides a relatively stable environment in which to invest because one investment can make up for another if one of these goes down in value while the other increases. It also provides higher return opportunities. Furthermore, you're creating your "mailbox money" by getting a return on a monthly, quarterly, or even sometimes, daily basis.

As an example, you can use a company like *Roofstock* to purchase a SFH (single family home) with little to no extra work. You're able to fully review the properties and its background, see current lease information and payment, and choose your funding options — all online! They have a team of experts that will walk you through every stage and assist you with picking the proper property for what your budget and outlook is. Remember, time is money! Don't waste your time on something you aren't well-versed on!

Real Estate — Passive

Now, if you're seeking a more hands off approach then you are seeking the passive lifestyle. This is where you are still earning your additional income, but not having to deal with any of the day to day and you're also not paying a property management company to do it for you. Wait, how is that possible? By being a passive real estate investor you are allowing yourself to share in the profit, and losses, of a property by "passing through" that income to yourself. Whether you've set up your investment account as an entity, you are still allowing yourself to reap the same benefits. You're also lowering your tax liability by utilizing the write-offs from what sources are being used.

You can now utilize platforms that allow you to invest in properties, the old fashioned way, but with a huge twist: You don't have to float the entire cost of the property yourself! There are plenty of options to collaborate with other investors and become a part-owner of a larger property.

With *Realtymogul*, you can invest as little as $1,000 and become a part-owner in a larger property. Pooling investment dollars allows you to 1) budget your money properly, 2) take less risks (not zero risk), 3) partner with other like-minded investors, and 4) minimize your output in selecting the right property. Again, do your research and reach out to the companies for additional information if needed. You also have options with REITS, or my personal favorite eREITS, which we'll talk about further on, but you have to envision what makes sense for you.

Rent What Someone Needs

When I talk to clients about how to create additional money, one of the things I say often is, *"Everyone needs something."* Which means, everyone is looking to use something for some...*thing*. Again, in the definition of the world wealth we have the word: possessions. If you're not using it, someone else will! Now, most will say, *"Well, if I don't need it, why can't I just sell it?"* You can, but what if you could make 3x, 4x, or even 10x the amount you would sell it for by renting it? Sounds better, right? Let's dig deeper....

You're probably not actually using that spare bedroom for anything other than storage, right? Why not fix the room up a bit and rent it out? What if your kids have now left the house to go off to college? That is a prime area to rent out in, especially if you live in a university city where students are looking to have reduced cost for their housing situation. Or, if you have some extra space in your apartment (but no older children), you can always opt for a roommate. Or, better yet, rent out your apartment in the summer while you're off on vacation (because you've utilized this book to increase your mailbox money!)

It just takes a small amount of time and effort to clean and de-clutter the space. You can advertise on lots of different websites like Airbnb or Zillow and set the rental terms yourself.

If you rent to a longer-term tenant, you'll be collecting a check with minimal extra effort on your part. In fact, short term tenants bring risks we'll talk about in a minute that you might want to stay away from.

Nowadays your rental space doesn't even have to be a room. You can put up a tent in your backyard and rent a camping experience if you live in a scenic area. (Seriously! This happens.) You can rent the whole backyard for a party space if you've got it decorated and have a barbecue pit and/or a pool. People will stay almost anywhere if it's interesting enough. You can even rent your garage space or parking space if you live in a busy city. The sky is the limit, but it's up to you to monetize what you own, but no longer use.

For reference, a client of mine is a personal trainer who turned his garage into a gym and charges clients to come to his home for training, but also rents out the space for other trainers to provide services to their clients. So, not only is he getting income from his clients and the trainers, but now he has a viable tax write-off on a property that he owns.

Starting to see the light? Monetize your possessions!

The first step is to check out the local laws. Call your housing authority or check out the local government website to find information about renting a room or space in your area. Your homeowners association may have additional laws regarding rentals as well, so check with them before you advertise.

Many city ordinances require renters to have access to clean running water and working plumbing. Some cities require a room to have windows large enough to be used as a fire escape – or even to have outdoor access. So, you'll need to make sure to check the laws before you rent. Again, *applied* knowledge is profitable.

Check out the fair housing laws at the U.S. Department of Housing and Urban Development (HUD), too. You'll need to create a tenant screening criteria form that will protect you if someone decides to file a discrimination claim against you. This lists everything to keep in mind when considering a prospective tenant. It's a little more work, but it may help you avoid a hefty legal fee. You can find many free examples of this form online.

Once you make sure you're legally allowed to rent space in your home, check your homeowner's insurance to make sure it's approved. Some companies don't have a problem, but others won't allow it – and some will raise your rates if you rent.

Tenants increase your liability and risk of property damage, so you might even have to get landlord insurance (which costs 15-20% more than homeowner's insurance). That'll save you from many headaches in the future! You never know when you may end up dealing with bad tenants.

Another way of renting your free space without having to deal with a lot of the admin aspect is to go the AirBNB route. This platform has proven to be quite useful for all kinds of renters because the difficulty or time-consuming aspects of renting are taken out of the equation. To have success with AirBNB, you need to make sure of a few things, first.

1. You need to limit your cancellations. They could be from a number of factors so ensure you're keeping up with detailed information on why.
2. Keep your calendar updated. The smallest changes in your calendar could lead to you being there when a tenant wants to rent if you haven't properly updated your calendar.
3. All requests you receive should be answered. Communication is a huge factor in deciding to go the AirBNB route.

A good way of making this a passive income and therefore something that requires less input from you is to hire a property manager, or someone that comes around and cleans up the area after a guest has left. This is less work and can therefore make it easier for you to have a new guest within a shorter period of time, thereby increasing your revenue. While it may cut into *some* of your profit — you're reaping the benefits of time and that is way more valuable.

If you own property, there are upkeep and maintenance expenses that are a part of owning real estate. These include taxes, insurance, taxes, repairs, and improvements, etc. When you rent a property, most times, these costs are fully covered by you. Therefore, you need to be covered for these.

Check comparable rental rates in your area to find out how much rent you can reasonably charge. You can use *RentoMeter* to check this out! Additionally, using a service like *Spare Room* or *Roomster* can help find a compatible tenant for your space.

"But what about my other possessions?" Oh, they absolutely apply too!

Do you own an antique car or a luxury vehicle you'd like to loan out? You can get setup with *Turo* and rent out your vehicle. Have clothes that you no longer wear? You can rent them out, as well. Tools? Yup! Machine equipment? Of course! A boat? Hot commodity!

The opportunities are endless, but it's up to you to decide what you're willing to rent out and how much effort you'd put into making it known. Again, everybody needs something for something, so do you have what they need?

Prescription: Applied Knowledge is Profitable

Do your dollars make sense?

A key factor that most individuals need to understand is that we all have our own knowledge, and that *applied knowledge* can truly be profitable. Now, we can't all be experts in everything and there are times you'll want to seek and find that knowledge elsewhere. This is one of those times. Let's take wealth as an example — *you can be wealthy*. Wealth is something which, with the right applied knowledge and effort, can be taught and created. But first you have to realize what it means to you! Everyone isn't going to have the same definition of what wealth is, but there is a common ground for some: *"The abundance of valuable possessions or money."*

Now, earlier we talked about what possessions you have and how they can be monetized — what I left out is the focus on your own mind. That initial concept of wealth, for most, leads us to think of worldly possessions, but most of us leave out the fact that our own minds, our knowledge, is what truly creates the wealth. Where does your expertise, knowledge, or current mindset lead to mailbox money that you may not have thought of? Or maybe you have, but you simply haven't acted on it. *The time is now.....*

Be Their Yoda

Many individuals have earned thousands upon thousands of dollars each month simply by teaching something that they know. Whether it be things such as how to play the piano, how to utilize certain computer programs, or how to speak another language — what you have in your mind is profitable. Indeed, these are all things that one can learn online nowadays, but that also means that you can be the one teaching them!

Now, before you dive off the deep end and launch your own online course there are many factors that you should consider first. Are you a person who is passionate about teaching this topic? Or do you just enjoy doing it? In any case, if you feel like you could be a great teacher of what you know, why not try it out? You may be surprised to find out just how much one can make with an online course.

One of the most common reasons why online courses are so popular is because they are extremely convenient. Instead of having to spend endless hours reading books (no pun intended) and then having to try and figure out where to go to practice the things you learned, you can simply turn on your computer, attend a class whenever you want, and can speak directly to others who are interested. For reference, there are a number of free courses online that allow you to practice and perfect your skills before getting started.

By selling your course, you only need to invest the initial time and capital to develop the course, and once it's posted, very limited effort is needed to keep it going.

Online courses are a popular passive income stream because they are incredibly flexible. Instead of relying on one's existing schedule and trying to make it all work when the time is limited, which can be often, online courses can fit around the customer's busy life. You can keep up with the class you are teaching whenever you have time at home, during a break in your shift, during the weekend, or even on your days off. This allows you flexibility since only a few hours here and there are needed.

If you have knowledge, or expertise, in an area and feel you can be a great teacher utilize Udemy to create you online courses. *Udemy* is a web based learning platform that allows you to access various courses and it is also a great platform if you want to upload an online course yourself. With this platform, you can create as many courses as you like, whenever you like, and for as long as you like. The beauty of Udemy is that every course has a forum for active discussion between instructors and students. Students can help each other with questions, and instructors can help students with problems.

If you want to use a less hands on approach, I recommend using *Teachable*. This online platform allows you to build your personalized online course, with video instructions and subscriptions services for your students, while providing you with all the tools and resources needed to be successful. This is literally a set and forget opportunity to mailbox money. After setting up your course, you simply have to check in for minor updates, add new content, hold live coaching sessions should you choose to, and bring your knowledge to life. Remember, your possessions, including your mind, is worth so much more than you think.

What's Your Story?

A s cliche as it is, you knew I was going to talk about publishing somewhere! Selling your story can be worth millions! Especially if you sell it on a platform like Amazon. They literally sell everything imaginable and books aren't any different.

An eBook can be classified as the future. The reason? It enables you to reach people who don't usually go to bookstores and people who are looking for books to access easily without waiting for delivery. When a person comes to know about your books, he or she may want to buy them right away, which means that waiting for the delivery may not be an option. An eBook, in this case, is a great resource to provide that alternative to the traditional method.

So, how much is your story worth? Or, what do you have to share? See, this is only 1 of a series of 3 books that will talk about the topics of wealth, passive income, and smart money. By opening up your platform to others not only are you monetizing the information you have, but you're also assisting in helping them get to the next level: A win-win for both parties involved.

But how do you get started? Well, the easy, and more expensive, way is by utilizing a publishing company. Yes, they are experts and yes, they probably have a bag of tricks and tools you didn't know about — but you also can do a lot on your own through self-publishing. You have a ton of resources literally at your fingertips by just opening an account with *AmazonKDP*

(Kindle Direct Publishing). Not only can you publish directly via the site, but you can also format your book, add your barcode, order your own author copies, and more. This also works for your paperback book should you want to add that additional option.

Now, if you're lost in time and simply don't have a clue where to even begin (Hello, writer's block!) then you can reach out to content creators on *Fiverr* to assist with your story. You can get with a ghostwriter who will either, create your entire book based upon what you tell them or you can literally record whatever it is that you want to write about and have them translate it into text for you. Remember, leverage those around you who can help you succeed in reaching your goals. Be sure to check the reviews and see their examples before getting started.

So, why publish your story? This is a great way to develop credibility and also boost your audience if you're in a specific field. In addition, you get an opportunity to test the waters and see if this is an opportunity to write more. In the sense of building a profit, you will want to focus on publishing a number of books to earn the value you seek. Although some say that having one book is enough, it isn't unless you're a celebrity or have already a large following and audience. You may make a few dollars here and there, but you will truly only make a solid *income* if you invest in enough books to the extent that the dollars all add up to a good profit. On the other hand, you could also leverage the social media you have, the story of your life, and can make an income by selling a book on those experiences.

Prescription: Be the Bank & Cut the Check

Money is more profitable in your hands

Do you remember hearing the old adage, "A dollar saved is a dollar earned"? Well, throw that out the window because that's not what's happening here. A dollar saved is *more* than a dollar earned when you *ARE* the bank! If you have ever heard me speak before I talk a lot about paying yourself first. That term goes hand in hand with realizing the potential in having multiple streams of income. If you are paying yourself first, you are allowing yourself an opportunity to have that dollar saved compound with additional interest. There is no reason why your money shouldn't be working for you — instead of you working for the money.

"When you become the bank you set the rules." You are monetizing your dollars further and exploring additional income options along the way. Not only are you putting back for your future or family, but you're also setting up your business, or businesses, to remain profitable for a longer period of time. Furthermore, you are cutting yourself a check — whether it be daily, weekly, monthly, quarterly, whatever! You are establishing a cycle of payments to yourself by monetizing your own dollars through passive income opportunities. But — you still have to do the work.

This isn't something new and it's been utilized by the wealthy for years. We simply needed to figure out how it fit into what we were trying to accomplish. It's time to start shifting the mindset in 3 particular ways:

Mindset Shift 1: Be the Bank or the Customer

Following the path of money leads you to two things:

Big Banks and the Wealthy

As a rule of thumb, there are two completely different rule books for how each operate. For most customers, they'll fall into the 3 different stages, financially: Foundation, Accumulation, and Preservation. That's how most of my clients come to me. They're either in the Foundation Stage, where they are just now building an understanding of their money, they're wanting to start a family, build a home, etc etc. Then there are those that are in the Accumulation Stage — building assets and growing their money to have them reach the Preservation Stage, or retirement. We are told to do the following:

- Put away as much as possible
- Put it away as often as possible
- Keep it there as long as possible
- Take as little as possible
- Take as much risk as possible

But the banks and wealthy utilize a different approach. Their rulebook is designed to provide the opposite of how we are taught and structured to capitalize on their value, assets, momentum, and overall willingness to provide credit to the customer.

Instead, their mindsets shift to:

- Get as much money as possible
- Get it as often as possible
- Keep it as long as possible

- Give you as little back as possible
- Take as little risk as possible (because its calculated)

A complete night and day difference, right? You're taught those rules so you can be a customer for life. Instead, apply *their* concepts and *your* rules to your own money and watch yourself prosper.

Mindset Shift 2: From Retirement to Financial Confidence

Have you seen some of the definitions of the word retire?

To put out of use; to move back (recede); or to withdraw. Retirement is leaving a job and ceasing to work — and for most — that means retiring your money and ceasing to allow it to work *for you*.

Retirement shouldn't be an ending point, but a side step into a new adventure. Stop seeking to "retire" but instead seek to become financially confident. Allow your money to work for you instead of you working for the money. If you do that you won't even have to worry about retiring because you never started working to begin with, ideally. Doing things you love is never a job, but a passion. Stop thinking about an end number and instead think of your comfort, peace of mind, and generational kickback.

"You can't create wealth if you don't understand the value of what it is to you."

Mindset Shift 3: From Uncertain to Abundance

Most commonly, people are uncertain about their finances and its future. But those that are wealthy, who take the time to realize the real value of their dollars, live in the abundance. Fear, worry, and doubt cast a shadow over an individual's finances and, either, makes them do too much with their money or too little. Financial behaviors is something I studied during my doctoral research and the amount of information is staggering. When you live in an abundance mindset, you realize that there is enough money for everyone and everyone should have their hands in something. Living in the abundance is realizing that all money is provided behind a value. If you offer the value *the money will come.* The banks have offered you, what you thought, was a value for years, but now that you know the difference — what are you going to do with it?

"I look at financial transactions as a movie and everyone's money plays a role. As the creator your choice now is whether you want your money to play the part of *their income* or *their expense.*"

-DR. KING MCCRAY

Personal Banker - Peer to Peer

R emember when I said, *"When you become the bank you set the rules?"* This is an exclusive opportunity to do so. This is where we can start to take control in our communities and do better. You know, actually *BE* the good in the world. I remember growing up and thinking, *"What do you mean you're going to charge me 400% to get a payday advance? Is that even legal?"* But unfortunately, it was. We all know there are hard times and when a loan is a purposeful option, but I'll be damned if I have to give up my right kidney just to make it to the next payday. If that *is* a struggle for you (shameless plug) you need to reach out so we can fix your financial situation. Be that as it may, if we have the additional income to provide a service back to our community, then let's do it in a proper way.

So, what does being the bank look like on a P2P basis? This is a personal loan where you're fronting the money through a third-party intermediary like *Prosper, Funding Circle,* or *LendingClub* and making money through the interest paid by your borrowers. Not only are you providing a service, but you can choose what loans you're investing in and how you're wanting to utilize that additional income from interest.

P2P loans are conducted online, so you don't actually have to meet with your borrowers in person. It's a more streamlined process, too, but in order to make a P2P loan work out, you need to do a good bit of research and learn all about the market. This is a passive income stream that requires both time and money up front.

The best way to handle this stream is to diversify: Invest smaller amounts over several different loans instead of loaning a large sum to one party. At Prosper, you can loan as little as $25. You'll want to investigate your potential borrowers, too. Make sure they'll be a good risk by checking their past loan history.

It does take time to master the techniques of peer-to-peer lending, so plan on a bit of effort at the beginning until you learn the ropes. You'll probably be dealing with Millennials, for example, who are five times more likely to fund their small businesses with a P2P loan than Generation X. Additionally, the terms are a bit more flexible, than your traditional bank, and gives you an opportunity to learn how to cut yourself a check from the interest by reinvesting on those same loans.

Risks with this income stream include being disorganized and missing payments – you have to keep up with all of those small loans and stay on top of borrowers. You might run the risk of a default if the economy takes a downturn, too (Hello COVID-19). In any case, you will want to make sure you have many streams of investments, not just one! This is how you can make sure to avoid being stuck in a situation where you have put all your eggs in one basket and thus where you lose all your investment at once.

You can go deeper with P2P lending and literally become your own personal banker by creating an entity and lending through your business. Of course, this raises the legal aspect of things and is more work on your end versus using an established platform and practice.

Use OPM (Other People's Money)

---◦---

"Live like no one else so you can *live* like no one else."
- Dave Ramsey

I want you to really take note of the quote above. While I may not always agree with Mr. Ramsey, I do believe this quote hits home for what a lot of people are wanting to do. If you live your life like no one else will, you can live a life like no one else does. You can truly start to increase your net worth by creating additional income streams and using a variety of approaches.

Now, when we start to talk about net worth we use the historical calculation:

Assets - Liabilities = Net Worth

But what if we flipped that on its head a little and started to do what the banks do to us: Use other people's money! That moment is when you decide to realize that some debt can be good — if properly used. Good debt is possible. Good debt is REAL! Open your mind to the fact that some liabilities are actually an asset if you use them for a specific purpose: To fund an alternative lifestyle and reward yourself with the financial benefits. The banks don't want to utilize their own capital so instead they use your money when you place your funds with them. You're incentivized to deposit your capital into the bank and then the bank uses *your* capital to invest and make *more* money. Do you see the cycle?

So, how can you utilize OPM to create passive income? By rewriting the rules and becoming the Bank of [Insert Your Name Here]. Seriously! Utilize the bank to fund your additional business ventures and keep more of your cash reserves for yourself to PAY YOURSELF FIRST! Any money that you receive should be paid to you first and compounded for additional interest. Again, good debt *is* real.

Let's take the SBA loan for instance. Most recently, because of the pandemic, SBA loans were given out at pretty attractive rates, although for very unfortunate circumstances. Be that as it may, it was a way to capitalize on an opportunity to create another business entity. Imagine receiving a $30,000 loan at a 3.5% interest rate over 30 years (360 months). That's a total repayment of about $18,418 in total interest over that time period if you paid to term. Now, this process only works if you have the cash flow to work it, your credit is in good standing (don't pile bad debt with good), and you have fully thought out your process and *planned thoroughly!*

Btw, what is cashflow?

Income - Expenses = Cashflow (NET)

So, if your cashflow is in a surplus (positive) that means you have the ability to invest or use your F-U Money to create additional opportunities. You've already paid yourself out of the income portion you received so you're left with a cash reserve, that *most* normally just leave in a bank, but now you have more options. For educational purposes, on average for the last century, if you're investing in a diversified portfolio, you can earn anywhere between 7% - 10% return (that's about 3.5% - 6.5% higher than the interest you're supposed to pay). You'll likely earn more than that if you're investing in a diversified portfolio which includes dividend paying stocks (which we'll get to), low cost ETFs, public utilities, and rebalancing your portfolio all while you're also utilizing the loan to pump money into your business venture.

Now, follow me— you've now used the bank to fund your "side hustle" that you'll in turn dump into a *tax-deductible account* which will lower your tax liability, increase your overall profit (by compounding interest), cashflow for additional expenses, and in a matter of years you can pay off the loan (with barely any interest paid) and continue to do the same cycle over and over again.

Remember, you're now rewriting the rules of what this banking relationship looks like. What role do you want your money to pay? Essentially, you're using someone else's money to build a new empire. The same exact formula most of the wealthy have been using for years.

Prescription: Hustle the Market

Two can play that game

Talk about your passive income streams! How much more passive can you get than socking your money into a high-yield savings account and just watching the interest add up, right? *insert Dad laugh*

WRONG!

While as kids we may have enjoyed this benefit, because most of us simply didn't know any better. We would go down to the bank, open up an account with our lawn-mowing earnings, and then watch eagerly as those pennies compounded. We were serious investors.

So long as the bank you chose is backed by the FDIC, your risk with this stream of income was pretty low. Just save up a few thousand dollars and aim for the highest interest rate possible. But, as we just learned — we got pimped!

While online banks can have interest rates that are 10 times more than your local brick and mortar bank (sometimes even more than that) this is a simple method of earning that just requires that initial investment of cash. The more you had, of course, means the more you earned in the end. The main problem that will arise is *when* the economy weakens. In that case, the interest rates will tend to drop and you won't get as much of a payout as you would otherwise.

But this low return versus what you can make by investing is the case a majority of the time so you can take your initial investment and spread it in the stock market instead!

The main times you would want to use a money market or high yield savings account is in the event that you just sold your positions and want to have cash on hand, need the cash within a short time frame (1-3 months), or simply need quick access to your emergency fund (Rainy Day Fund).

Obviously, investing has its challenges, but by learning the information, you can set yourself up for success. There are resources you can use that will allow you to learn more about investing, like the Ostrich app, for example. *Ostrich* is a financial literacy application (for Android and Apple users) that allows you to do financial challenges, read about common financial mistakes, find accountability partners, or simply gain more financial information. The tools and the resources available have an easy-to-understand outline and have tremendous value for those seeking information.

So, how can you truly hustle the market? Let's see....

REIT Me Up!

This section is going to outline The Passive Real Estator 2.0 — *REIT (Real Estate Investment Trust)*. It's just a fancy term for any company that owns and handles real estate. They usually own and/or manage commercial properties (either the physical property or the mortgage on that property) and they tend to focus on a specific group of properties, like medical care, shopping centers, or hotels. You know, things that are going to be around for a while.

A REIT is like a stock share. They're structured so that they pay little or no income tax so long as they pass most of their earnings along to their shareholders. You buy a REIT, just like any other stock on the market, and earn dividends several times a year as with other high-yield dividend stocks.

Retail REITS (shopping malls and freestanding retail businesses) account for about 24% of investments in America – that's the biggest investment by type in the country. When you're thinking about investing in a REIT, you need to look at the whole retail industry. Is it healthy and likely to stay so – or are things looking rocky? For example, following the Covid-19 crisis, investing in this may not be the best choice just yet. (Or is it?) Individuals have now learned to see the benefits of online shopping as it is a much more efficient and comfortable way to shop rather than having to drive for an hour to the next mall. However, you can also look at places that you know people have been dying to visit since the beginning of the pandemic and can take the opportunity to invest in these!

Remember the REIT firm is getting its income from the rent of its tenants, so if you've got a shopping center or business that's got a high turnover rate, it's probably not going to generate as much income as you'd like. Instead, you want to look at the firms that have a low turnover rate or that have had the same owners for many years now.

You might think about aiming for traditionally "safer" real estate investments like grocery or home improvement stores. Keep in mind, also, that a lot of shopping is shifting to online so alternative REIT options are available with apartment complexes, rental homes, etc. That shopping mall may not even be in existence in ten or twenty years. So, think about the basics. What do people need, and how certain can you be that the demand will still be there for those exact companies in just a few years from now? Can it be automated? Is it likely to disappear as an industry altogether soon? If so, steer clear!

As stated previously, there are also residential REITs, which focus on apartment buildings and manufactured housing. With this type of REIT, you'll want to look at the location. For example, the best apartment markets are where there are fewer homes available, like in large urban centers. The largest residential REITs tend to focus on areas like this. Now, *that* is what you'll make the most money on!

You should also look at population and job growth. As long as the apartment supply in your market stays low and demand is increasing, your residential REIT should perform well. In other words, will the place you are investing in even have demand? Will there be people to use the places you've invested in? If the job offers have been stagnant and people aren't moving to the area, try out other places.

Healthcare REITs invest in the real estate of hospitals, medical centers, nursing facilities and retirement homes. This is probably going to be one of the investment areas to watch as our Baby Boomers grow older and require more skilled care. Similarly, more and more people are getting sick, unfortunately. Obesity and heart disease are on the rise, and therefore these bring on huge costs to hospitals and medical facilities. Although a very unfortunate reality, it is an opportunity for investment.

However, remember that the success of the REIT is tied to the healthcare system. So long as the healthcare funding remains questionable, so do these REITs. Look for companies with a lot of healthcare experience, not new companies that have yet seen the hardships of the industry.

There are also office REITs who handle office rentals. There are 4 basic questions you may want to ask when investing in this area:

- How high is the unemployment rate?
- What are their vacancy rates like?
- What's the economy like in the area you'll be investing in?
- How much capital does the REIT have?

Think of investing in "economic strongholds." In other words, it's better to have a bunch of average office buildings in DC than to have prime time space in Detroit.

Dividends from a good REIT can even increase yearly, so you might just end up with a growing stream of dividends over time. How good does that sound? You're also likely to receive your payments quarterly, monthly, and even sometimes daily.

There's a bit of research involved with this stream, as with any stock purchase. You want to be sure to pick the best REITs that will increase your earnings instead of dropping in value. You'll also need that initial outlay of cash to get the ball rolling, and so this is something you can get access using what you just learned: OPM!!! *Leverage the bank.*

One way to minimize your risk is to buy into an Exchange-Traded Fund (ETF) that diversifies by investing in lots of different REITs instead of sinking everything into just one individual trust. These often have lower risk ratios so you can gain exposure to real estate trading without as much risk as investing in an individual company.

You do need to do your homework with a REIT or an ETF. Even though it's considered passive income, you can lose big if you choose the wrong ones. You'll want to start analyzing these companies like you did for regular stocks. It takes a bit of time and effort before you can pick out the best choices.

A tough economy can take a big bite out of your income stream as well. If your REIT doesn't create enough income, it might reduce the dividend or cut it out entirely. That could be disastrous because a tough economy is just when you'll need that passive income to come in. By also strategizing and using a newly formed eREIT (electronic Real Estate Investment Trust) you can set yourself up for a diversified real estate portfolio. The term eREIT was created and coined by, *Fundrise*, the first online investment platform to create a pathway to private real estate.

Traditionally, individual investors have been limited to investing in public stocks and bonds, while institutional investors have consistently outperformed public markets by investing in alternative assets like private market real estate.

Fundrise offers a real alternative to the traditional REIT market. A Fundrise eREIT invests in debt and equity real estate opportunities that match each eREIT's particular goals. For example, the objective of the Income eREIT is to earn consistent cash flow for investors. To achieve this, the Income eREIT has invested in more debt investments than equity investments. As a reminder, there *is* good debt and good debt *does* pay.

There are many ways to approach real estate investing, but no matter what kind, or how, the most important step is to ask the right questions and do the right research.

Run Up the Dividends

Show me the money!

If you'd like to invest your money in a company with *dividend-yielding stocks*, you'll receive a dividend check a few times a year without having to do anything other than put in your initial investment. These dividends depend on how many shares of stock you own, so it's a good way to invest a larger sum of money.

You'll also want to put in some research effort for this passive income stream. Choosing the right stocks is essential. You want something that's going to increase in value over time, not decrease. This is something that you can learn. You can do so by following our online courses, for example, that are based around teaching you just how to spot the rising stocks and those that you should be selling. As an educational example, Starbucks tends to increase in the summer because people want to drink cold, iced drinks. Similarly, shares and the value of companies like Zoom increased in the pandemic because everything went online, and thus the value of the service itself grew as its usage did. You have to be smart with your investment!

Spend at least a couple of weeks investigating each company you're considering, so you're familiar with their financial statements and can tell whether or not they're likely to go up in value. If you're unsure how to read a financial statement, reach out so I can educate you on how that process works.

So, why are dividend stocks good?

There are three primary reasons behind why dividend stocks are fantastic options:

- Long-term Returns – Some people may look at dividend stocks and their payout over the short-term before dismissing them as worthless. However, in the long-term, these stocks have been proven to account for a major percentage of total investment returns on the stock market. Let's take a look at the infamous FTSE 100 Index as a prime example. Bloomberg reported that, between 2006 and 2016, the FTSE 100 companies returned around 17% when *not* including dividends in the calculation. Add dividend stocks to the mix and that goes up to 67%!

- Passive Income – Well, of course! Dividend stocks have the ability to bring in passive income for the investor and a sizeable one, at that, over the long term. Not only this, but it allows you to take your regular cash payments from the dividends and reinvest them in your portfolio. That's passive income that can create further income!

- Protection – The stock market is volatile, we all know that, however, it is important to realize that in times of market volatility dividend stocks often fall less than growth stocks. This is because, on average, companies that offer dividends have good reputations and are established names, meaning investors turn to them in times of trouble.

For those of you that are my novices try *Exchange Traded-Funds (ETFs)*. These are investment funds that hold assets such as stocks, commodities, and bonds, but they trade like stocks. They're easy to understand and inexpensive compared to regular dividend stocks. They cost less than mutual funds and are easy to liquidate when you need to.

A big risk (besides picking the wrong stocks) is that stocks and ETFs can drop in value significantly if the market takes a downturn (as it did early in the global pandemic). Nonetheless, it is still an investment worth making and is one that is relatively easy to learn. You can, for example, easily learn how to read the stock market simply by learning to read charts and following the news. Or you can outsource this part to a financial advisor, like myself, who can help walk you through the understanding and investing pieces.

To further throw an additional nugget out there for my people — if you really want to capitalize on dividend growth look at where your tax bracket currently is. Tax rates are historically lower than normal and if you're single (making less than $39,375) or married (making less than $78,751) as of the 2019 tax year, you owe no tax on your qualified dividends and long term capital gains. That's a huge win for those who qualify. Now, if you're over that financial threshold than it is more in your favor to place your dividend paying stocks in an after-tax account (Roth IRA) seeing as how tax rates are more than likely to rise and you'll pay more in income tax in the future. Remember, dividends can be taxed as ordinary income *or* as capital gains depending on whether it is qualified or not. Qualified dividends are those paid by U.S. corporations and certain qualified foreign companies where you meet a minimum holding period requirement.

According to the Internal Revenue Service, you must hold a stock for 60 days during the 121-day period that begins 60 days before the ex-dividend date to meet the requirement. The ex-dividend date is the first day new shareholders aren't entitled to receive the next dividend payment. Qualified dividends are taxed at a maximum rate of 15%.

So, if you're likely to be in a higher tax bracket than the normal

15% long term capital gains tax, and don't want to pay the difference, shift your mindset. And if you must use a DRIP (Dividend Reinvestment Plan) utilize a tax-sheltered account to maximize on your earning potential and offset *some* of your tax liability.

Supersize Your Options

Let's weigh the options…

O*ptions* trading is the act of purchasing and selling stock or various other financial instruments at prearranged prices in hopes that the underlying price of these instruments will move either up or down. For example, if you purchase an option on a particular company's stock, you're purchasing the right, however unconfirmed, to sell or buy that stock in the near future at a set price. If you're right then, you win; if you're wrong, you lose. An option is a derivatives contract that gives the buyer the right but not obligation to buy (*call*) or sell (*put*) the underlying stock at a predetermined price by a predetermined date. When the buyer uses this right, it is called "exercising."

The writers of options, called option sellers, are obligated to give their shares or an equivalent dollar amount if assigned. Assignment happens when the buyer exercises their contract. To avoid assignment, the writer must buy to close their position. A seller buys to close when he or she buys the identical contract that was written. To be clear, the writer must buy a contract with the same strike price and expiry.

Any contract $0.01 in the money will be automatically exercised by your broker, though some phone applications allow you to disable the feature. It is best to manage your trade before expiration, or more than one hour *BEFORE* the markets close.

For someone just beginning to explore the world of options trading, it is important to know the basic terms. Two of the most important terms when it comes to trading options are the *premium paid* for an option and the *strike price*. The premium paid for an option is usually determined by the security's intrinsic value (the security's worth). This is usually determined by various factors such as current market rates, inflation, economic growth and other economic factors. The strike price, on the other hand, is what the option can be sold for when it is exercised.

Calls are another important term to understand. There are various calls, but let's focus on a long call. A long call is one where you buy call options from investors who think that the stock price will go appreciate (up). These offer an unlimited potential for profit as the value goes upward. If you experience a loss, the maximum is the option price as even if it goes up or down, you will not lose less than the original price you paid for the option.

For a call, the contract is in the money if the underlying stock is trading above the strike price. Excluding other factors for ease of learning (commission costs, etc.), when your contract is in the money- be it a call or put- you are in a profitable position. The expression "*in the money*" refers to an option which has intrinsic value– so an in-the-money call option means that the option holder (not writer) has the opportunity to purchase the security below the current market price.

" *At the money*" is when strike and market price for underlying are the same.

"*Out of the money*" means that the underlying is *BELOW* your strike for a call, and *ABOVE* your strike for a put.

For example, let's say there is a call contract for AAPL, 150, MAR 31 2021. Let's say Apple is trading at $122. This person would be out of the money, because it would make no sense to buy the option for $150, when they can buy it at market for $122.

Conversely, let's say one is considering a put for AAPL, $110 MAR 31 2021. They are out of the money, as it would make no sense to sell Apple for $110, when they can sell it at market for $122.

Finally, if your options expire out-of-the-money (OTM), the options are worthless, and you lose your premium paid.

A strike price refers to the price that will be paid for the option regardless of the way it goes (up or down). In other words, when the cost of the stock goes up or down, this is the price that you will be when you choose to exercise the option. So, for example, if you buy an option with a strike price of $45 USD but the value of the stock goes up to $60 USD, you get to buy the stock for $45 USD even though the value is now $60 USD. Similarly, if the value goes down to $40 USD, you can still choose not to exercise it, which would mean that you lost only the option price (which is how much you paid for the option itself).

Options are risky! They are much riskier than stocks, as you could lose your entire account in a matter of mere minutes, provided you have no exit strategy in place. Again, utilize your resources and seek financial assistance with a professional in that area should you choose it.

For educational purposes, if I invest $10k in a stock, it will have to go to $0 for me to lose everything. If I put $10k in an option, the underlying could fall $4, and I would lose everything right then.

Options deal with leverage. One contract is worth 100 shares of the underlying, so just as gains add up quickly, so do the losses. Options are, however, less expensive than stocks, as 100 shares x $122 ($12,200) is far greater than an $800 contract that covers the exact 100 shares.

It is important that anyone who is new to options trading understands that there are a number of risks associated with this type of investing. Because options have expiration dates, it can become difficult to exercise the call option before it becomes invalid. Also, because trading options expose you to risk by fluctuating in price, it can be hard to make a consistent profit from them if you don't have the experience to determine when to execute the option.

In any case, options are quite complex. Therefore, if you have no experience with the stock market just yet, stick to simpler concepts for now.

Bond to the Top

How can you utilize bonds to work your way through a passive income stream? By using a bond ladder. This is a portfolio of fixed-income bonds that mature over a period of years at different times. It is also an investment option that lets you decrease your reinvestment risk by minimizing your exposure to fluctuating interest rates.

Let's say you buy a five-year bond at a fixed interest rate - but two years from now, interest rates are going up. Your bond is still chugging away at that lower rate and there's no way to change it. However, if you have different maturity rates, you might be able to roll over some of your bonds and take advantage of that better rate. You can take the same amount of initial investment and stagger your maturity times so you're more likely to be able to profit from the market.

Another example: You purchase a 2-year bond and get a 1% yield on that. You also purchase a 4-year bond for a 2% yield, a 6-year bond for 2.5% yield, and an 8-year bond with a 3% yield. In two years, when the first bond matures, you reinvest the proceeds in a new 8-year bond with 3% yield – and continue this practice as your bonds mature (assuming interest rates stay the same or increase, of course).

The average financial advisor might suggests buying a minimum of ten securities for diversification. The idea is to take the total amount you're planning to invest, with the goal being to extend your ladder as long as possible. One would suggest a minimum of $100,000 to be invested with ten rungs(steps) of $10,000 each.

One benefit to having at least six rungs is that you can easily build a ladder that will generate monthly income, since each bond will pay out twice a year. You'll also want to consider the spacing between rungs. The longer the ladder, the higher your income is likely to be, since those are the bonds that will give you higher yields. Of course, going long tends to increase your risk, as we discussed previously. You may reduce your income a bit by buying shorter-maturing bonds, but it'll be safer in the long run.

A ladder may also be useful when yields and interest rates increase because it regularly frees up part of your portfolio so you can take advantage of new, higher rates. If all your money is invested in bonds with a single maturity date, you might be able to reinvest at higher yields, but your bonds might also mature before rates rise.

Just like a physical ladder, you build this one with different material. In this case, different types of individual bonds, mutual funds, or ETFs. As each one matures, you just reinvest the principal in new bonds with the longest term you originally chose for your ladder. Bond ladders do come with risks, of course. And since bonds are not backed by the federal government (like corporate bonds), you might lose your principal.

Before building a bond ladder take into consideration the following 6 options that could allow for this passive income opportunity to make more sense for you.

1. Use high quality bonds — Ladders are intended to provide predictable income over time. Using higher-quality bonds

can give you that possible predictability you're looking for. Be sure to check the ratings, as they may frequently change, and be comfortable with choosing A rated bonds or higher.

2. Avoid the highest yielding bonds — Historically, using a similar, higher yielded bond indicates the market is signaling a downgrade or is perceiving the bond to have more risk than others. Having a lower price and a higher yield should signal a red flag, except a potential exception of municipal bonds (where buyers often pay a premium).

3. Hold until maturity — This should go without saying. If you're creating a strategy that is designed off of the maturity dates then you should have a temperament that can ride the ups and downs of the market. If you don't have that strong stomach — this may not be the option for you. Maximizing the regular income and risk management is by holding the bonds until term. Not only could you risk income by selling early, but you could incur transactions fees or miss out on market timing and hit further interest rate risks.

4. Callable bonds are a no-no — The beauty of a bond ladder is knowing when interest is paying you and predicting that particular income to reinvest it or use it for other purposes. If a bond is called prior to maturity the interest payments cease and your principal is returned to you — well before you want it to be.

5. Time and frequency are important — A ladder with more bonds requires a larger investment but will also create a greater range of maturities. Should you choose to reinvest, you have more time to review the interest rate environment and gain more opportunities.

6. Know your limitations — Simply put! Ask yourself, or your advisor, whether you have the assets to create such a bond ladder. Do you have the time to structure, time to research, and the willingness to manage a bond ladder?

So, just like stocks and REITs, you'll want to own many different bonds to diversify your risk. You can find a bond ETF just like an REIT ETF, that will give you a portfolio of bonds you can build a ladder from. This will greatly decrease your risk of a single bond hurting your returns in the long run.

Prescription: Money on Autopilot

Create sustainable income

During my studies I ran into a fairly rich individual — not wealthy, but rich. There is an honest difference between someone being wealthy and someone being rich. This individual was rich because he had a massive amount of money coming in from various sources, but he wasn't *wealthy* because nothing he was doing was sustainable. See, that's the key difference between the two — being rich merely means you have a ton of money but that money has an expiration date. Being wealthy means not only is your money sustainable, but your assets are as well. Building a true generational foundation is about how to create sustainable income — *money on autopilot.*

See, this rich individual built a ton of businesses, but each that required a massive amount of capital, a ton of attention, and in industries that were, either, not sustainable or not able to be easily duplicated. In our talks he realized that he needed to hire me to assist him in managing what he had going on, but he was so busy trying to build what he thought was generational wealth for his children. Now, I want you to take note — when you're on the airplane the flight attendants make a very, very good statement: **"Put your own mask on first, before you assist others."** This is a concept I teach often to my clients and how we structure their wealth — you have to focus on you *first* before you try to build for someone else. In doing so, you're creating a foundation and allowing your money to now run on autopilot so you can do other things.

Once we had the opportunity to work together and really deep dive into his businesses, he realized that they were all being ran manually and couldn't sustain the cashflow he was wanting. Just as much money as he had coming in — he had a fair amount going right back out in expenses. We had to go back to the drawing board, literally shut some businesses down, and recreate a sustainable, duplicated process that worked in his favor. Now, he has his children running these sustainable businesses and has created succession plans for each so that they may all be inherited properly.

So, how do you get your money to run on autopilot? By creating sustainable and duplicated businesses that can be ran minimally and with the least amount of exposure to you. Structuring your business under the proper entity is a starting point, but seeing what options lie ahead, could be the difference maker in your overall profit.

As you do continued research on what industry, product, or service you'd like to adhere to — review what has been around and has stood the test of time. I'm going to show you just a few of those options and how you can incorporate them to have your money running on autopilot and continuing to receive mailbox money.

The Infamous Wash & Fold

The arrival of the laundromat opened up a whole new world to many people who are looking for ways to supplement their income. For the basics, a laundromat is an industrial laundry service that can bring you a lot of income once the initial investment is done. It is more like a large warehouse where clothes are stacked in bulk and sorted on a conveyor belt. A self-service laundromat or coin laundromat is a business unit where clothes are cleaned and dried without too much personalized assistance– and that's the key, the human capital needed is low, thus there is no need to pay staff. For that reason, laundromats tend to be the perfect example of a *sustainable* passive income source.

Though, laundromats do have their advantages and disadvantages. For example, the main advantage is that customers do not need to worry about being stressed about speaking to an employee or business owner and vice versa. This is an advantage for an individual who may not necessarily be a people person, but want to supply a service *for the people.* In addition, the lack of a staff, as stated above, allows you to limit your capital and liability exposure. Keeping more of your capital allows you to reinvest in the business by buying another building, utilizing more machines, marketing and advertising — just to name a few. Running a self-service business is a crucial component to keeping the money flowing on autopilot. By installing different sizes of washing machines, not only are you tapping into the clientele who the normal services, but even those with machines at home may need laundromat services for larger items, therefore expanding your client base. Again, add in the prescriptions you've already learned: *Monetize your possessions, rent what others need, use other people's money, etc., etc.*

To open up your laundromat, you will need initial capital to invest, so where could you possibly get the money? This is where you can use other people's money and structure a loan or use profit from your other businesses and investments. You will need to find an area in which your business is needed, done through thorough research, in the middle of a city area that is prone to tourism. You can also look into university halls (dormitories) as these tend to be big money-making machines. Once you have the area then you can supply and find the necessary machines, building space, etc. If you structure things properly within the laundromat you also have a smaller passive income opportunity. Doesn't laundry need detergent? Maybe add in some softeners? What about the customers who don't want to fold their own clothes? Charge for the additional services, monetize on the opportunity, and leverage the relationships by having one or two employees, if needed.

The point is to create a business that will sustain with time and gives you as little issues as possible. Yes, have reserves for mechanical issues and your low cost expenses, but a majority of this business funnel is on autopilot. You can bring this further and invest in a vending machine as well, which is actually the next item on our list of stabilized business opportunities to your mailbox money.

America's Favorite Machine

Vending machines are everywhere and are considered to be a very popular business venture. A vending machine is similar to how you'd want to receive your money: At the push of a button. It's something that you can buy to place your products on, in, and take money out of whenever you want. The truth is, if set up properly, vending machines can be one of the most lucrative business opportunities. They offer great profit potential, as long as you're willing to invest the time and effort into them at the beginning, but once they're set up — *autopilot!*

When you think about it, the vending machines that you see all over the city are the perfect example of low-effort money-making. Of course, once the initial investment is made, the funds needed to keep the business going are very low. Aside from having to purchase the items which are being sold in the machine itself, you don't have very much to do! And those items can be purchased at wholesale value so your return is higher.

But where do you place your vending machine? Well, they are used in retail stores, movie theaters, fast food restaurants, convenience stores, takeout counters, airports, and bars, business centers — to name a few. A vending machine usually sells items like candies, drinks, snacks, sandwiches, coffee, and other instant foods, but they can also be used to sell items that you may have from another business venture. Do you have essential oils or lotions that you sell?

I've seen hotels that allow for these items to be placed inside the vending machines if hotel residents weren't interested in the "generic" products that are behind the counters. I've even seen a vending machine that sells lashes on the go — seriously, eye lashes! When your vending machine is not in use for food, or lashes, they sometimes have a small area for displaying messages. Imagine, using your vending machine as a way to also advertise, either, your own additional business venture or sell space to other companies. That's a two for one opportunity! Ideally, your vending machine can be used to sell just about anything.

If you want to start working on a vending machine business, it's important to get the right licenses, permits, insurance, etc. Of course, this depends on where you reside, so a quick Google search will help you out with this. You must also have a business plan that explains how you will be distributing goods and how much money you expect to make, along with a marketing plan so you can visualize your ideas and to help make them come true. Remember, failing to plan is planning to fail.

One of the largest industries in the country happens to be the food industry. There's hardly a department store or major chain that doesn't have a vending machine in it that allows you to buy their beverages and snacks. This makes vending machines an excellent way to supplement your income if you happen to own your own business or even own multiple. Feel free to partner with like-minded individuals to expand your operations. Consult with your local barbers or hair stylist, local physicians or dentist, or even tap into a local gym or school.

Storage Wars

It takes time, effort, persistence, motivation, and some skill, to build a profitable and sustainable business. When you focus on what people *need* versus what they *want* you can start to take a unique approach to your income streams. Think of it this way — if you have what people need then you, and your business, continue to stay relevant.

With the world's population continuing to grow, there has been a rise in the demand for self-storage facilities. Whether it is people moving, lifestyle transitions, travel, or life events like divorce, death in the family, retirement, etc. — each of these are now creating a demand. Like most other passive income opportunities, this will require start-up capital, your time, commitment, and some patience. But, with time, a lot of your additional ongoing tasks and systems can be automated, outsourced, and duplicated to build more streams.

If you think about self-storage units and how it incorporates with market demand, even in a recession these have a good track record of success. First, you must identify the target market and what niche will be suitable for you as this can save you a lot of time and money. Self-service storage can be suitable for many uses, and you do not want the luxury of serving a risky clientele in a questionable area. The target market that you identify can be influenced by certain factors. You can consider the location for your business, consumer storage trends, security measures to protect you against theft and regulations. In short, you should look at these few simple factors for your niche:

- How suitable is the location?
- Where is your nearest competition and who is their target?
- What additional services can you offer?
- How can you stand out against your competition?

In doing so, you're now targeting the ideal customer you'd like to serve. You will be actively involved in the business operations for the first 3-6 months, but again, once up and running things can be outsourced or automated. For example, we recently rented a storage unit and the entire transaction was done online. We've never met an employee, when we went to the unit we simply opened it up and our lock was already there, and this specific property closes at a certain time so we can only access between those business hours (which is an ideal option for added security).

Do consider the financial investment with this passive income opportunity. While the profit and upside is tremendous, the start-up is no small feat. The land space could account for up to 30% of your initial cost. Think of it as $25-$40 per square foot for a single storage or $75 per square foot for a multi-unit. The key is to have an organized budget when you are first starting operations. As a rule of thumb, it is more in your favor to buy someone out then to build your own storage unit. Starting from scratch isn't always the key to success — why reinvent the wheel?

You'll also have to look at the overall expenses to get the needle moving. Some of these expenses do include, registering your business, licensing, insurance, equipment, accessories, and of course, marketing.

Now that I have given you an idea of the risk, what does the reward look like? It looks like you enjoying that newly minted mailbox money. With an average cost of $60/month for your smallest unit (let's say a 5x10) and $125/month for a larger unit (10x15), simply renting a few units can be extremely lucrative — especially if you're flipping the profit into other passive streams or hustling the market for compound interest. Let's say you rent 20 small units (20 x $60) and 15 of your larger units (15 x $125/month) then we're looking at a total of $3,075/month (of course less any expenses and paying yourself first). There are major businesses making billions of dollars because they chose to duplicate, automate, and reinvest their business.

Again, scalability, time, and competition are your biggest factors in taking the risk, but you'll have to educate yourself on this opportunity. This isn't a one size fits all option, but the reward can be truly endless and allow for that money to continuously flow on autopilot.

Finale: "Make it Make Sense"

W hen it comes to building passive income streams that will help you experience true financial confidence, I want you to think of it in this terminology, *"You'll catch more fish with multiple lines in the water."*

Don't be afraid to venture into other avenues or launch multiple businesses in different industries or niches! Understand that leverage is a key component to getting you to where you want to be. Additionally, partnerships are okay. Pool your money together, structure the business entity properly, and just truly create. Be sure to research each market thoroughly or hire an expert to both prepare and mentor you throughout the process. (*Yes, I have openings on my calendar.*)

There's no limit to the amount of money you can make — there's only a limit to what you restrict your thoughts to. The sky is the limit. Use your resources, scale the business if need be, or simply focus on small investments here and there. Either way, make a conscious effort to create.

With a little time, a couple dollars, and a lot of determination, you can generate a nice, solid foundation of mailbox money that you can wake up to for years to come, but as a favorite saying of mine, *"Just make it make sense!"*

About the Author

A driven and professional business pioneer, King has successfully owned and operated a private financial advisory & wealth planning firm and managed over $450 million in assets for corporations and small business owners alike for nearly 15 years.

King pulls from hands-on experience and education to intricately understand how the market can affect your financial portfolio, how marketing can make your business sink or swim, and how the advancements in technology are a trend worth following. Staying ahead of the industry's frequent changes, the financial literacy of households and successful marketing techniques are King's sixth sense.

From working at prestigious Fortune 500 management firms to opening his own practice in 2007, King has represented businesses, artists, designers, musicians, athletes, and hardworking Americans, large and small.

A serial entrepreneur and community activist, King fulfills multiple speaking engagements throughout the year to reach as many people as possible and inform them of their options for uncovering their financial confidence. He excels at embracing his background and education to cater to audiences as a dynamic and motivating keynote speaker, openly providing descriptive insights into his personal failures, successes and passion for helping others.

In an ongoing effort to give back, King teaches youth workshops on "Financial Freedom & the Pathway to College," a financial series that centers on misguided youth and their adventures in the new financial world. He also sits on the board or serves as a participating member of a host of organizations, including the National Association of Professional Agents (NAPA), Phi Beta Sigma Fraternity, Inc., Blacks in Government (BIG), YMCA, Soles 4 Souls, Big Brothers Big Sisters and more.

King holds a Bachelor of Science in Business with a concentration in Marketing and Business Law as well as a Master of Business Administration from University of Phoenix. He also holds a Master of Science in Management, Strategy and Leadership from Michigan State University, as well as a Ph.D. in Business from Kingston University - London. His certifications include Accredited Investment Fiduciary (AIF®) & Federal Retirement Consultant (FRC^{SM}).

Residing in Central Florida, King spends his rare free time with his family, playing golf or basketball, and traveling the world.

For speaking engagements or consultations please visit: www.creatingyourwealth.org or contact our administrator via email at admin@creatingyourwealth.org.

Resources

Need an additional overview of the resources listed in this book. Check the list below depending on what opportunity fits you best!

Real Estate:

Pockets: www.biggerpockets.com

PropStream: www.propstream.com

Roofstock: www.roofstock.com

RealtyMogul: www.realtymogul.com

Fundrise: www.fundrise.com (eREITs)

Renting Your Space/Possessions:

RentoMeter: www.rentometer.com

Spare Room: www.spareroom.com

Roomster: www.roomster.com

Turo: www.turo.com

Online Courses:

Udemy: www.udemy.com

Teachable: www.teachable.com

Self-Publishing:

AmazonKDP: www.kdp.amazon.com

Fiverr: www.fiverr.com

P2P Resources (Be the Bank):

Prosper: www.prosper.com

Funding Circle: www.fundingcircle.com

Lending Club: www.lendingclub.com

www.ingramcontent.com/pod-product-compliance
Lightning Source LLC
La Vergne TN
LVHW051200080426
835508LV00021B/2716